Dear Parent:
Your child's love of reading starts here!

Every child learns to read in a different way and at his or her own speed. Some go back and forth between reading levels and read favorite books again and again. Others read through each level in order. You can help your young reader improve and become more confident by encouraging his or her own interests and abilities. From books your child reads with you to the first books he or she reads alone, there are I Can Read Books for every stage of reading:

SHARED READING
Basic language, word repetition, and whimsical illustrations, ideal for sharing with your emergent reader

BEGINNING READING
Short sentences, familiar words, and simple concepts for children eager to read on their own

READING WITH HELP
Engaging stories, longer sentences, and language play for developing readers

READING ALONE
Complex plots, challenging vocabulary, and high-interest topics for the independent reader

ADVANCED READING
Short paragraphs, chapters, and exciting themes for the perfect bridge to chapter books

I Can Read Books have introduced children to the joy of reading since 1957. Featuring award-winning authors and illustrators and a fabulous cast of beloved characters, I Can Read Books set the standard for beginning readers.

A lifetime of discovery begins with the magical words "I Can Read!"

Visit www.icanread.com for information
on enriching your child's reading experience.

A nod and a wink to the late great Dave Keenan
—S.K.

"Change is the law of life."—JFK
Thank you Rick, Jeanne, and Jeff for
helping me change and put together this book.
—C.K.

Picture Credits
The following photographs are courtesy of the John F. Kennedy Presidential Library and Museum, Boston: page 27, John F. Kennedy in his Dexter Academy football uniform; page 32, JFK inspecting the *Friendship 7* Mercury space capsule—Photographer Cecil Stoughton. White House Photographs.

The following photograph is courtesy of the Library of Congress: page 28, Jackie Bouvier Kennedy and John F. Kennedy cutting their wedding cake—Photographer Toni Frissell.

The following photographs are © Getty Images: page 26, Kennedy with his PT boat crew, Mr. and Mrs. John F. Kennedy; page 27, Rose Kennedy with five children in 1921, Jack at age ten, the Kennedy clan in the 1930s; page 28, Lieutenant John F. Kennedy in the cockpit of Torpedo Boat *PT-109*, John F. Kennedy and Jaqueline Bouvier sailing—Photographer Hy Peskin; page 29, campaign button, Kennedy and Nixon at the first televised presidential debate—Photographer Paul Shutzer, ticker-tape parade—Photographer Frank Hurley, *Life* magazine cover—Photographer Leonard McCombe; page 30, JFK playing peekaboo, with Caroline—Photographer Ed Clark, John F. Kennedy Jr. playing under his father's desk, President Kennedy with Caroline, John Jr., and Macaroni; page 31, JFK in his rocking chair, President Kennedy talking to Nikita Khrushchev—Photographer Paul Schutzer, Kennedy meeting with his advisors.

Designed by Jeff Shake
Library of Congress Control Number: 2017930904
ISBN 978-0-06-243259-9 (trade bdg.) — ISBN 978-0-06-243258-2 (pbk.)

17 18 19 20 21 SCP 10 9 8 7 6 5 4 3 2 1
❖
First Edition

I Can Read!™

READING 2 WITH HELP

JOHN F. KENNEDY
the Brave

by Sheila Keenan

pictures by Chin Ko

HARPER

An Imprint of HarperCollinsPublishers

His last name came from
his rich father.
His middle name came from
his powerful grandfather.
Nobody even used his first name.
Everybody just called him Jack.

One day, he would be called
Mr. President.
John Fitzgerald Kennedy became
the thirty-fifth president
of the United States.
Getting there was like an adventure
book he had read as a boy. . . .

Jack was a skinny, sickly kid.

But he was a Kennedy.

His Irish-American father

was very clear on what that meant.

"We want winners in this house."

So scrappy Jack kept up

with his eight brothers and sisters.

Jack often had health problems.

Whenever he was sick, he read.

He liked hero stories
and history books.

He read the newspaper every day.

Jack Kennedy wanted to know

what was going on in the world.

Jack joined the navy during World War II.
He was in charge
of a small patrol boat, *PT-109*.
One dark, moonless night,
an enemy warship plowed right
through Jack's boat.
PT-109 was ripped in half!

The crew was thrown into the ocean.

Jack saw a sailor who was badly hurt.

Jack grabbed the strap of the man's

life jacket in his teeth.

He towed the sailor as he swam.

Jack and his crew swam for hours

before they reached land.

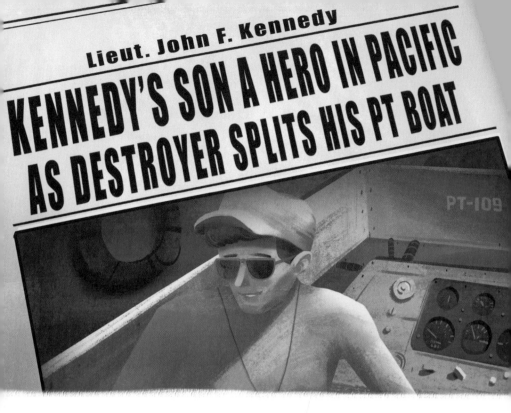

Jack Kennedy was a hero,

just like in the books he had read!

He won medals.

His picture and story were all

over the newspapers.

The next year another Kennedy

made headlines.

SON OF
KENNEDY
KILLED
IN ACTION

LOST ON FLIGHT

Jack's older brother, Joe, died.

Jack was changed by the war

and his brother's death.

He wondered what to do next.

How could he make the world

a better place?

His father had an idea: go into politics.

Jack ran for Congress
from Massachusetts.
He greeted workers at factories
and fish markets.
He shook hands with voters at delis,
diners, barbershops, and ballparks.

Jack won the election.

While he was in Congress,

he married a newspaper photographer

named Jacqueline Bouvier.

In 1960, Jack Kennedy
ran for president.
He had bold ideas for the future.
He did well on the first
presidential debate ever shown on TV.
Voters liked what Jack had to say
and how he said it.
But he was Catholic.
Some people believed a Catholic
should not be president.
On election day,
Jack proved them wrong—
but it was a *very* close race!

John F. Kennedy, 43,
became the youngest person
and first Catholic
ever elected president.
The lively, charming Kennedys
moved into the White House.
First Children Caroline and John Jr.
played in the Oval Office.

The First Lady restored

the White House

to show off its history.

The president met with his staff

and world leaders.

He faced many challenges.

The United States competed with
another country, the Soviet Union.
Both wanted to be the most powerful
country in the world.
The Soviets sent the first person
into orbit around the Earth.

So President Kennedy built up

the US space program.

He vowed to put a man on the moon.

Jack was not going to lose

the space race!

But a more deadly race was going on.

The Soviets put missiles in Cuba.

They could easily strike the United States.

War might break out!

Kennedy said the missiles had to go!

The Soviet leader said no.

Neither one wanted to seem weak.

No one would back down . . . in public.

President Kennedy knew that war
would be terrible.

So he secretly worked things out
with the Soviets.

The missiles were removed.

Kennedy also faced a crisis at home.

Black people in the United States

were not treated fairly.

They couldn't always live, work,

eat, shop, or go to school

where they wanted.

They marched on Washington

for equal rights.

Martin Luther King Jr. gave
his "I Have a Dream" speech.
President Kennedy listened.
He drafted a civil rights bill to protect
black Americans.

Jack Kennedy did not live to see man
reach the moon
or his civil rights bill pass
or his children grow up.

President Kennedy was shot and killed
on November 22, 1963.
But his ideas live on:
"Ask not what your country
can do for you;
ask what you can do for your country."

Timeline

1917
Kennedy is born on May 29, in Brookline, Massachusetts

1940
Graduates from Harvard College

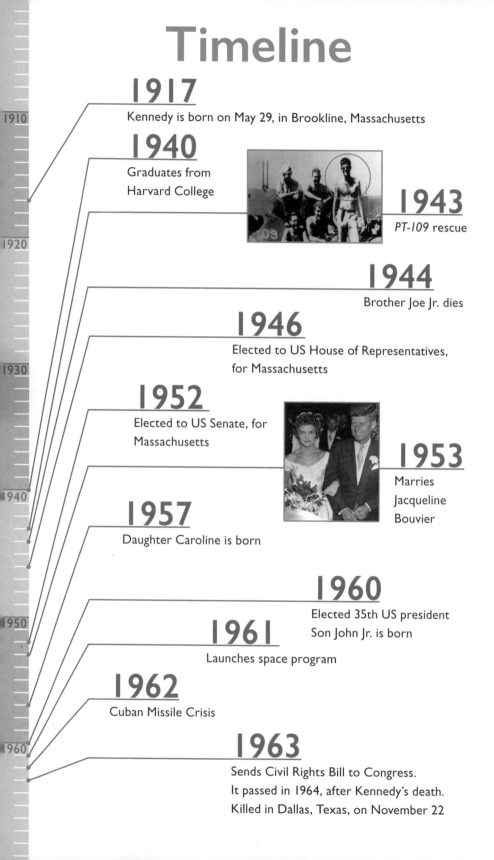

1943
PT-109 rescue

1944
Brother Joe Jr. dies

1946
Elected to US House of Representatives, for Massachusetts

1952
Elected to US Senate, for Massachusetts

1953
Marries Jacqueline Bouvier

1957
Daughter Caroline is born

1960
Elected 35th US president
Son John Jr. is born

1961
Launches space program

1962
Cuban Missile Crisis

1963
Sends Civil Rights Bill to Congress.
It passed in 1964, after Kennedy's death.
Killed in Dallas, Texas, on November 22

1910
1920
1930
1940
1950
1960

JFK's early years

Jack in his football uniform in 1926

Rose Kennedy (seated) with five of her children in 1921. From the left are Joseph Kennedy, Jack Kennedy, Kathleen Kennedy, Rosemary Kennedy, and Eunice Kennedy.

At age ten in 1927

The Kennedy clan in the 1930s. John F. Kennedy is standing, the second from the left.

JFK as a young man

Jack as a naval lieutenant on board the torpedo boat he commanded in 1943

Jack and Jackie go sailing in 1953.

John F. Kennedy marries Jackie Bouvier in 1953.

Running for president

Meeting Richard Nixon during the first general election presidential debate ever in America. Nearly seventy-four million Americans tuned in to the television broadcast.

THE KENNEDY INAUGURATION

LIFE

JANUARY 27, 1961 20 CENTS

Presidential nominee John F. Kennedy and his wife, Jackie, riding up Broadway in New York City in a ticker-tape parade in 1960

Life magazine cover showing the new president and his wife riding to the White House

The young family

President Kennedy playing peekaboo with his baby daughter, Caroline, in 1958

John Kennedy Jr. playing under his father's desk in the Oval Office at the White House in 1963

President Kennedy with Caroline Kennedy, John F. Kennedy Jr., and Macaroni, Caroline's pony, in 1962

President Kennedy at work in the White House

President Kennedy met with many world leaders. Here he is in 1961, meeting Nikita Khrushchev, the Premier of the Soviet Union.

President Kennedy sitting thoughtfully in his rocking chair

President Kennedy holding emergency talks with his advisors during the Cuban Missile Crisis in 1962.

Looking toward the future

President Kennedy built up the space program. Here he is looking at the space capsule *Friendship 7* with astronaut John Glenn in 1962. Glenn was the first American to orbit the earth.

Civil-rights leaders met with President Kennedy after the March on Washington for Jobs and Freedom in 1963. Martin Luther King Jr. is the second from the left.

Learn more about President Kennedy and his family:

John F. Kennedy Presidential
Library and Museum
www.jfklibrary.org

White House biographies of
presidents and first ladies
www.whitehouse.gov/1600/Presidents